How to Do a Health and Safety Audit

CANCELLED

Also available

In this series: Health and Safety in Early Years Settings

How to Avoid Illness and Infection
Lynn Parker
1-84312-299-5

How to Keep Young Children Safe
Lynn Parker
1-84312-301-0

Other:

The A–Z of School Health: A Guide for Teachers
Adrian Brooke and Steve Welton
1-84312-830-4

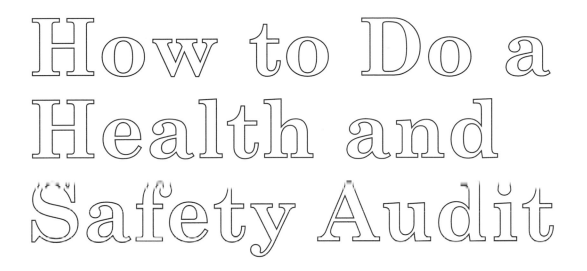

How to Do a Health and Safety Audit

Lynn Parker

 David Fulton Publishers

David Fulton Publishers Ltd
The Chiswick Centre, 414 Chiswick High Road, London W4 5TF

www.fultonpublishers.co.uk

First published in Great Britain in 2006 by David Fulton Publishers

10 9 8 7 6 5 4 3 2 1

David Fulton Publishers is a division of Granada Learning Limited, part
of ITV plc.

British Library Cataloguing in Publication Data
A catalogue record for this book is available from the British Library.

ISBN 1-84312-303-7

Typeset by FiSH Books, Enfield, Middx.
Printed and bound in Great Britain

Contents

Foreword

Working with young children is both a pleasure and a privilege, but with each of these comes responsibility. One key area of responsibility is health and safety. Managers of all early years settings need a clear understanding of what is required, both to fulfil their duties, and to impart knowledge to their staff and those training with them. These books will help achieve this.

One of the first things students undertaking training in early years are introduced to is safe practice, both for themselves and for the children they will work with. The importance of taking responsibility for personal safety is discussed in this series along with how to observe and supervise children appropriately. The *Health and Safety in the Early Years* series presents three accessible books covering all the main aspects of health and safety in early years environments under three main topics. These books will be of considerable use to managers, qualified practitioners and students on a range of courses.

The series can be read as a set, perhaps to support assignment work or within staff training, or as stand alone texts. Managers will find examples to help them support the development of their staff, as the books present information that will both consolidate and extend understanding for most readers. Useful chapter summaries and best practice checklists help give an 'at a glance' reminder of what should be happening today and every day. The use of bullet points for emphasis throughout the books works well, and each book includes a comprehensive list of references and/or contacts.

In *How to Do a Health and Safety Audit* health and safety legislation is clearly set out along with guidance on writing policies and procedures. A useful template for creating a health and safety audit has been provided together with lists of questions suitable for supporting practitioners in carrying out an audit of the safety in their setting.

This series highlights why revisiting understanding, and updating knowledge of this area of responsibility is so important.

Sandy Green – Early Years Consultant

Introduction to the series

This book is one of a series of three addressing the issue of health and safety within the early years setting. Those who work with young children have a responsibility for providing a safe environment to ensure their well-being.

The National Standards provide a baseline for the provision of quality child care but you also need to comply with national legislation covering health and safety, food hygiene and fire safety.

This book provides an introduction to the subject of health and safety. It aims to inform you of the relevant legislation and regulations; and to provide practical audit tools, advice for parents and a template of a health and safety policy that can be adapted for use in your setting.

CHAPTER 1

The essentials of health and safety legislation

Introduction

By providing the right environment and taking appropriate precautions it is possible to prevent people being harmed or becoming ill through their work. Complying with health and safety legislation is not expensive, time-consuming or complicated; it is about encouraging everyone to become safety conscious and creating a safety culture. To achieve this, problems have to be recognised, assessed, agreed and acted upon. This chapter provides an introduction to the current regulations that form the basis of health and safety within the UK.

The essentials of health and safety in early years settings

Health and safety is about preventing people from being harmed at work or becoming ill by taking the right precautions and providing a safe environment. Duties under the legislation apply to both employers and employees in early years settings, including those who, like contractors, come onto the premises to do repairs and maintenance.

Responsibilities for health and safety in early years settings are based on the Health and Safety at Work etc. Act 1974 and its associated regulations. As far as is reasonably practicable, the health and safety of staff, children, parents and visitors while on the premises or out on organised outings must be protected. Risk assessments and audits must be carried out as part of measures taken to minimise or control risks. Everyone has their own roles and responsibilities.

Responsibilities of the employer

Overall responsibility for health and safety remains with the employer, who provides as far as is reasonably practicable for the:

+ health, safety and welfare of staff;

+ health and safety of children in the early years setting and on off-site visits;

+ health and safety of visitors to the early years setting and of volunteers involved in any activity.

The employer must also:

+ have a health and safety policy and arrangements to implement it;

+ assess the risks of all activities, and introduce ways to manage these risks and inform employees of what to do.

While it is possible to delegate safety tasks to individuals, the ultimate responsibility always stays with the employer.

Responsibilities of the employees

Staff also have responsibilities under health and safety law and must:

+ take reasonable care of their own and others' health and safety;

+ co-operate with their employers;

+ carry out the activities in a safe manner in accordance with any training and instruction they have received;

+ inform their employer of any serious risks that they have identified.

Assessment of risk

All activities that are performed on the premises must be assessed for their level of risk. Once this has been done, the employer must decide how that level of risk can be reduced or eliminated.

Employers' liability insurance is compulsory. If the local education authority (LEA) is not the employer, the certificate should be clearly displayed on the premises. While public liability insurance and professional liability insurances are not compulsory they are often considered to be essential in practice.

You should also display the health and safety law poster in the premises – this can be obtained from HSE Books (ISBN 0 7176 2493 5).

National care standards

The revised *National Standards for Under Eights Day Care and Childminding* were published in September 2003, with an addendum in October 2005. These 14 standards form the framework for Ofsted inspections under the *Children Act 1989*. Early years setting providers must comply with these standards and the supporting criteria that explain how facilities can show compliance to the childcare inspectors.

National Standards relating to health and safety

✚ Standard 1 – Suitable person – requires the person to be able to plan for and provide a safe and healthy environment.

✚ Standard 4 – Physical environment – requires that the premises are safe, secure and suitable for their purpose.

✚ Standard 5 – Equipment – requires that all equipment conforms to safety standards.

✚ Standard 6 – Safety – requires the registered person to take steps to promote safety in the setting and on outings to make sure proper precautions are taken to prevent accidents.

✚ Standard 7 – Health – requires the registered person to promote the good health of children and to take positive steps to prevent infection spreading and take appropriate measures when they are ill.

✚ Standard 8 – Food and drink – requires food and drinks to be properly prepared.

Ofsted inspections

Once a setting is registered as a day-care provider, Ofsted childcare inspectors visit at least once every two years. The purpose of such visits is to check whether the early years setting still meets the National Standards and remains suitable for the provision of day care.

Ofsted may visit at other times:

✚ to check on actions given at an inspection;

✚ to consider a change of conditions of your registration if requested by yourself;

✚ when something about your registration has changed, such as an extension to the premises;

✚ if a parent or other person provides information to Ofsted that questions the suitability of the early years setting to provide day care.

Relevant legislation

What is health and safety law?

The basis of British health and safety law is the *Health and Safety at Work etc. Act 1974*. This sets out the general duties of employers, which are qualified by the principle of 'so far as is reasonably possible'. The law requires what good management and common sense would lead most employers to do anyway: to look at the risks and take sensible precautions to prevent and manage them.

The *Management of Health and Safety at Work Regulations 1999* (*the Management Regulations*) generally make more explicit the requirements for employers to manage health and safety under the act and apply to every work activity.

Actions employers are expected to make

The main requirement is to carry out a risk assessment, which should be as simple and straightforward as possible.

While the overarching legislation is the *Health and Safety at Work etc. Act 1974*, there are a number of other regulations that require you to take action in response to certain hazards.

Health and safety legislation applicable to all places of work

Management of Health and Safety at Work Regulations 1999

Employers are required to carry out risk assessments, make arrangements to implement necessary measures, appoint competent people and arrange for appropriate information and training to staff.

Workplace (Health, Safety and Welfare) Regulations 1992

These regulations cover a wide range of basic health, safety and welfare issues such as ventilation, heating, lighting, workstations, seating and welfare facilities.

Personal Protective Equipment at Work Regulations 1992

This requires employers to provide appropriate protective clothing and equipment for their staff. PPE covers a wide range of items including protective clothing for carers such as disposable aprons, gloves, eye and facial protection as necessary.

Provision and Use of Work Equipment Regulations 1998

This requires that equipment provided for use at work is safe for the purpose intended. It should be maintained, and staff provided with information and training on its use.

Manual Handling Operations Regulations 1992

These cover the moving of objects by hand or bodily force. As far as is reasonably possible staff should avoid any manual handling that will result in risk of injury. Assessment of tasks should be made to include the ability of the individual, the load and the task.

Health and Safety (First Aid) Regulations 1981

These require the employer to provide adequate and appropriate equipment, facilities and personnel to allow first aid to be given to staff if they are injured or become ill at work.

Health and Safety Information for Employees Regulations 1989

Employers are required to display a poster telling staff what they need to know about health and safety (see p. 3).

Employers' Liability (Compulsory Insurance) Act 1969

Employers are required to take out insurance against accidents and ill health to their staff so that they have a minimum level of cover should someone make a claim against them for compensation.

Reporting of Injuries, Diseases and Dangerous Occurrences Regulations 1995 (RIDDOR)

Employers are required to notify certain occupational injuries, diseases and dangerous events to the Health and Safety Executive. Incidents should be recorded in an accident book and include:

✚ death of a person;

✚ major injury where someone is taken to hospital or needs immediate medical attention;

✚ over-three-day injuries where someone is off work for a period of time related to an accident or injury at work;

✚ specific diseases.

Electricity at Work Regulations 1989

This requires that people in control of electrical systems make sure they are safe to use and maintained in a safe condition. The regulations are intended to control the risks around the use of electricity at work.

Control of Substances Hazardous to Health Regulations 2002 (COSHH)

The law requires employers to assess the risks from hazardous substances and take appropriate precautions to control exposure to hazardous substances to prevent ill health.

Food Hygiene Legislation

There are three relevant key laws around food hygiene in Great Britain:

The *Food Safety Act 1990*

The *Food Safety (General Food Hygiene) Regulations 1995*

The *Food Safety (Temperature Control) Regulations 1995*

The *Food Safety Act* requires that you:

+ must not sell food unfit for eating;

+ must not sell food that is not what customers expect in content or quality;

+ must not describe or present food in a way that is false or misleading;

+ must not cause food to be dangerous to health.

The *Food Safety (General Food Hygiene) Regulations* require that:

+ you have effective food safety management systems in place to produce food safely, and health is not put at risk;

+ basic hygiene principles are followed in relation to staff, premises and food handling.

The *Food Safety (Temperature Control) Regulations* stipulate:

+ those stages of the food chain that are subject to temperature controls;

+ that certain foods are kept at appropriate temperatures;

+ which foods are exempt from specific temperature controls;

+ when the temperature controls allow for flexibility.

Best practice checklist

+ Be aware of the hazards and risks involved where you work.

+ Undertake a risk assessment.

+ Write down your health and safety policy.

+ Make sure you have employers' liability compulsory insurance and display the certificate.

+ Include health and safety on induction for new staff and have regular annual updates.

+ Take advice from an expert if you are unsure about any aspect of health and safety.

+ Encourage safety awareness and safety practices in everyone.

+ Report all work-related accidents, diseases and dangerous occurrences.

+ Consult staff on health and safety matters.

+ Clearly display the health and safety law poster.

SELF-REVIEW ACTIVITY

Develop an induction programme to introduce new staff in your early years setting to the subject of health and safety.

You might:

+ look at the key issues on health and safety and consider the regulations as they relate to your own premises;

+ consider what are poor safety attitudes and how these can be turned into good safety attitudes;

+ emphasise particular topics such as security, fire safety, first aid or moving and handling as it relates to working with young children;

+ create a quiz to cover the key points covered in the session;

+ undertake an assessment of your setting with new staff to get them to identify hazards and assess risks.

End-of-chapter summary

Those working in early years settings have a legal duty to provide children with a safe environment by working to high safety standards. This chapter has presented an introduction to the current legislation and regulations and how they relate to the *National Standards for Under Eights Day Care and Childminding*.

CHAPTER 2

Developing a safety culture in your setting

Introduction

This chapter looks at the requirements necessary for implementing a health and safety policy in the workplace. Not only the premises but also the equipment used within it need to be maintained in a good state of repair to ensure they do not become a hazard to children, staff and visitors. A health and safety policy affects all activities within the early years setting. You must use it to ensure that hazards have been identified and risks assessed to protect those on the premises. Involving staff in its development and implementation encourages a positive health and safety culture.

Key requirements for implementing health and safety

Key elements of a health and safety policy

A health and safety policy is a document specific to your setting that states how you manage health and safety. It is unique to the individual premises and provides information on who does what, when and how they do it.

If more than five people are employed, then you must by law have a written statement of the health and safety policy. This should be written and revised by those working on the premises, as managers and staff all have experiences that are worthwhile to the development of such a policy. The policy should be reviewed and revised on a regular basis, e.g. annually, and also after any emergency situation or if there have been operational or organisational changes.

An alternative to writing your own policy is to use the services of a private health and safety consultant, but it is extremely important that you make sure they prepare a policy specific to your premises and involve all the staff.

Most organisations set out their policy in three sections:

✚ a statement of intent which sets out your commitment to managing health and safety effectively and what you want to achieve;

✚ an organisation section which states who is responsible for what;

✚ an arrangements section which contains details of what you are going to do to achieve your aims.

There may be sections of a health and safety policy that you require help with. Involvement of employees and safety representatives in identifying problems and seeking solutions can be helpful. Health and safety covers a wide range of issues, which you should be able to assess for your premises, but you may feel that on specific issues you or your employees lack sufficient knowledge or experience. The following checklist provides some questions to consider when it might not be obvious that outside help is needed.

Checklist for identifying the need for outside help		
Question	**Yes**	**No**
Do you have evidence of exposure to something that might cause harm?		
Are you unsure whether you have identified *all* the hazards involved in your work?		
Are you uncertain if they are a risk to staff?		
Are you unsure whether you have done everything necessary to control the risk?		
Are you thinking about introducing new working practices, equipment or processes that might impact on staff health and safety?		
Are rates of sickness and absence a problem?		
Do you think you should analyse the proportion of sicknesses and absences that might be work-related?		
Have you noticed a pattern of ill health or accidents you can't explain?		
Have staff reported symptoms of ill health that they think are work-related?		
Are you aware of reports of health and safety problems in other early years settings?		
Have you had any 'near miss' incidents?		
Have you had any compensation claims?		
Have you any member of staff who is returning to work who has particular health and safety needs?		
Are you unsure about what the health and safety law requires you to do?		

If you answered yes to any of the questions, you should consider the following points:

✦ Have you analysed the problem as fully as possible?

+ Do you think you need help?

+ Have you asked your staff and their representatives?

+ Is there anyone in the nursery who can help you?

+ Do they need some extra or refresher training before they help you?

+ Have you checked other sources of information for help?

+ Have you compared your practices against other early years settings or what is considered good practice?

The following health and safety specialists may be able to help:

+ health and safety management

+ engineers

+ occupational hygienists

+ occupational health professionals

+ ergonomists

+ radiation protection advisers

+ non-ionising radiation advisers

+ physiotherapists

+ microbiologists.

Should you need help, it is worthwhile preparing a written specification covering what help you need, such as:

+ the problem and why you cannot manage it yourself;

+ information about your nursery;

+ what you want the specialist to do;

+ what you would consider to be a successful outcome;

+ the resources you can offer, and a named contact point to support the adviser;

+ when you want the work to be done by;

+ how and when you want reports;

+ any other relevant information.

Advice before you write a health and safety policy

The health and safety policy is a plan that sets out how you are going to manage health and safety. It sets out your commitment to health and safety, and informs your employees of their responsibilities and the steps that staff need to take to meet their duties.

Before writing the policy it is important to understand your legal duties and appoint a competent person to manage health and safety on your behalf, depending upon the size of the premises.

There is a legal duty to undertake a risk assessment to identify any aspects of the premises that could cause harm to:

+ the children

+ yourself

+ your employees

+ members of the public

+ the environment.

The outcome of the risk assessment will then form part of the arrangements section of your policy.

What to put in a health and safety policy

The *Health and Safety at Work etc. Act* states that you have to put your policy in writing and then put it into practice.

The statement of intent

The statement of intent is in simple terms your general aims with regard to your staff's health and safety, and should be signed and dated by the most senior person. There is no set format as to what to include in the statement, but they are often only one page long.

Most statements of safety policy will state:

+ your commitment to ensuring the safety of your staff, children, parents and visitors to the early years setting and anyone else whom you think you have a responsibility to;

+ who is ultimately responsible for health and safety in the early years setting;

+ which staff have special responsibilities for aspects of health and safety, giving their names;

+ that all staff are responsible for taking care of their own health and safety and that of the people they work with;

+ that you recognise the legal duties of the early years setting and that you will provide a safe working environment, equipment and methods of work;

+ the organisation and arrangements in place to support the policy.

Some of the ways in which you can bring the policy statement to your staff's attention are by:

+ including it in the staff handbook;

+ providing it at induction;

+ including a copy with the contract of employment;

+ posting it on your intranet site (if you have one);

+ posting it on noticeboards;

+ making the duties in the policy part of the staff's workplace objectives.

The organisation

Responsibility for health and safety rests with the employer, although many duties can be delegated to managers, and the statement should show clearly how duties are allocated. This is your structure for safety and key job titles should be named and their responsibilities defined.

You can identify:

+ who will do the risk assessments;

+ who will do the workplace inspections;

+ who will ensure the safety of specific tasks or work activities or areas of the early years setting.

This section may include a diagram or flow chart showing the management structure and the responsibilities of:

+ the manager;

+ supervisors or team leaders;

+ employees.

The duties of the competent person you have designated should be mentioned in this section along with their contact details.

The arrangements

In the arrangements section you should describe the systems and procedures for making sure employees' health and safety in the workplace is maintained. All of the hazards should be addressed, including procedures for carrying out risk assessments and dealing with fire and arrangements for providing training and first aid.

This section is very important and should be user-friendly. This can be achieved by listing hazards alphabetically, by rooms or specific areas.

 *A **hazard** is anything in your early years setting that could cause harm either to people or the environment. A **risk** is the chance, however large or small, that the hazard could cause harm.*

The risk assessment will have highlighted areas that pose a risk and the measures you currently have in place. The additional arrangements you will make to control or minimise the risks you have identified should be set out in the arrangements section of your policy and include:

+ staff training;

+ using signs to highlight risks;

+ improved safety equipment such as gloves or aprons;

+ replacing hazardous chemicals with environmentally friendly alternatives;

+ improved lighting or anti-slip flooring.

Attention should be focused on the greatest risks or those risks that could affect the most people.

Risk assessment

The important things to decide when doing a risk assessment are whether the hazard is serious and whether you have precautions in place to keep the risk of injury small. A good example of this is electricity: it can kill but the risk of it doing so in the early years setting is unlikely provided that the building conforms to building regulations and equipment such as kettles does not have bare wires or worn flexes.

Looking for the hazards

Walk around the premises and see what could reasonably cause harm. Ignore trivial issues and concentrate on hazards that could result in serious harm or affect several people, for example:

+ poorly maintained floors or stairs that people could slip or trip on;

+ materials or chemicals that are a fire risk;

+ moving parts of equipment;

+ hot surfaces such as food trolleys;

+ parking of vehicles that block fire exits or are a hazard to children and parents;

+ poor wiring to electrical appliances and fittings;

+ dust;

+ lack of guidelines on manual handling procedures;

+ noise;

+ poor lighting;

+ extremes of temperature.

In addition:

+ ask staff if they can think of any other hazards that might not be immediately obvious;

+ look at the manufacturer's instructions on equipment.

Identifying people at risk

Individuals do not need to be listed by names. Simply group together those who work or use the building:

+ cleaners, contractors, maintenance workers, admin staff;

+ those who may be vulnerable to certain risks and need particular attention
    - children
    - visitors
    - students
    - inexperienced staff
    - staff working in isolation
    - expectant mothers;

+ members of the general public, especially if you hold fund-raising events.

Evaluating risk

Evaluate the risks and decide whether the existing precautions are adequate or whether more can be done. Think about how likely it is that each hazard could cause harm; this will identify whether you need to do more to reduce the risk. Even after all precautions have been taken, there is some risk that remains. What you need to do then is categorise each significant hazard remaining as high, medium or low risk.

Ask yourself if you have done all the things that the law says you must do:

+ Have you met the standards set by legal requirements?

+ Does what you have done represent good practice?

+ Have you reduced the risk as reasonably as practicable?

It is important to remember that the basic aim is to reduce all risks as much as possible.

Drawing up an action list

If things need to be done, you should draw up an 'action list' and prioritise any risks that were identified as being a high risk and/or those that could affect the most people.

When taking action consider:

+ Have you provided adequate information, instruction or training?

+ Are the systems/procedures that are already in place adequate?

+ Is it possible to get rid of the hazard totally? If not, how can the risks be controlled so that harm is unlikely?

The principles of controlling risk should be applied in the following order:

1. Try a less risky option.

2. Prevent access to the hazard.

3. Organise work to reduce exposure to the hazard.

4. Use personal protective equipment.

5. Provide an area where washing or first aid can be undertaken.

Recording the findings

If five or more people are employed there must be written records of the significant findings of your assessment. Your employees must be informed of the findings.

A risk assessment checklist should show that:

+ a proper check was made;

+ you asked who might be affected;

+ you dealt with all the obvious significant hazards;

+ the precautions are reasonable and the remaining risk is low.

Written records are useful for future reference and can help if an inspector asks what precautions have been taken, or if you become involved in any civil liability action. They also act as a reminder to keep an eye on any particular hazards and precautions.

When writing your report you can refer to material that is already published on health and safety procedures, which includes:

+ guidance from the Health and Safety Executive;

+ manufacturers' instructions;

+ your own safety procedures;

+ your arrangements for fire safety;

+ your general arrangements and policies.

Reviewing the assessment

You must review the assessment when new equipment, new building or temporary structures, substances and procedures which could lead to new hazards, are introduced to the premises. You do not need to amend your assessment for every new change, but you should make sure that there is an annual review to check that the precautions for each hazard still adequately control the risk. If the precautions are not adequate, you should identify the action needed to be taken and record the outcome of that action.

Developing a safety culture

Safety means freedom from danger or hazards, it doesn't just happen but is the result of individual efforts. The attitude of staff and employers to health and safety can have an impact. Poor attitudes, such as the following, can lead to danger:

+ cynicism

+ fatalism

+ showing off

+ laziness

+ recklessness

+ overconfidence

+ forgetfulness

+ ignorance

+ carelessness.

Good safety attitudes help ensure workplace safety. Good health is a safety plus, as fatigue is a frequent factor in accidents.

Best practice checklist

+ Have a written health and safety policy.

+ Make sure there are arrangements for monitoring and reviewing the policy.

+ Provide training on health and safety for new employees and update their knowledge annually.

+ Know what to do if there is any health and safety emergency.

+ Keep written records of accidents, including those that are reportable under the *Reporting of Injuries, Diseases and Dangerous Occurrences Regulations 1995 (RIDDOR)*.

+ Think fire safety – have regular testing of alarms and evacuation procedures.

SELF-REVIEW ACTIVITY

The five steps to assessing risk in the workplace are:

1. Look for the hazards.

2. Decide who might be harmed and how.

3. Evaluate the risks and decide whether the existing precautions are adequate or whether more can be done.

4. Record your findings.

5. Review the assessment and revise it if necessary.

Read again the section on risk assessment and then, using the five steps to assessing risk, walk around your early years setting, identify any hazards and discuss these with your colleagues to see if they agree with you.

End-of-chapter summary

Health and safety encompasses a wide range of topics but they all require you to promote a culture of safety and compliance with the current legislation within your setting. Undertaking a risk assessment provides information about the setting that can be used to establish an action plan. This can in turn be prioritised, implemented, measured, reviewed and then used to periodically audit the system overall.

CHAPTER 3

Aiming for quality and auditing the early years setting

Introduction

Quality is defined as *the standard of how good something is when measured against other similar things*. There is a constant search for excellence and quality, especially when considering the care provided in the early years setting. With the introduction of national standards there is a baseline for comparison between different child care providers. There are also a number of Quality Assurance schemes that help early years settings raise standards of the child care that is provided. Such schemes are programmes designed to raise standards above and beyond those national standards set by Ofsted and show a commitment towards increased knowledge and continuous improvement to practice.

This chapter looks at the issues around quality, audit and standards and how a safety culture can be encouraged.

Quality issues

Quality is very difficult to measure and the meaning of the word varies depending upon your own perspective. Managers, staff and parents all have different priorities in the assessment of quality because of the different roles they have in the early years setting. There is no single, comprehensive indicator of a quality service, though one of the best-known theoretical models is Maxwell's division into six dimensions of effectiveness, efficiency, equity, acceptability, accessibility and appropriateness (Maxwell 1984).

Dimensions of quality – definitions

✛ Effectiveness – the extent to which objectives are achieved; ideally you should be able to measure outcomes

✛ Efficiency – 'value for money'; how to make the most of the resources available

✛ Equity – equal treatment or access

✛ Acceptability – the manner and environment in which care is provided

✛ Accessibility – to include times, location and suitability for those with disabilities

✛ Appropriateness – relevant to the needs of the children or priorities of the local LEA

While these definitions may be desirable attributes, they might not be applicable to every situation or environment.

Recent attempts to define quality have concentrated on *effectiveness* in that it gives the feeling of achieving a desired goal or of meeting a defined need. However, quality improvement activities often require investment in staff time or resources.

Quality assurance schemes help to raise standards of care and demonstrate commitment to best practice, and to continuously improve practice. Current quality assurance schemes include working in partnership with parents to make sure that individual children's needs are considered and met. They build upon the national standards that are used by Ofsted when inspecting early years settings. They are also a means by which staff are able to update their knowledge in child care and show continuous improvement to their practice. There are a number of quality assurance programmes that are endorsed through the government initiative of Investors in Children. On successful completion, a Quality Assurance Certificate is received that can be displayed in the child care facility.

Encouraging a positive health and safety culture

Under the health and safety legislation an employer has a legal duty to consult with staff when preparing and implementing a safety policy. The benefit of involvement of staff in developing the health and safety policy is a sense of ownership. Along with this, staff may be more likely to comply with the practices because they understand and agree with the reasoning behind their implementation. The person who is actually doing a job is often the best person to advise whether the safe working method will work. This is often referred to as a positive health and safety culture.

The four 'C's of a positive health and safety culture are:

+ competence

+ control

+ co-operation

+ communication.

Competence involves:

+ assessing the skills needed to carry out all tasks safely;

+ providing adequate instruction and training for all staff;

+ arranging access to advice and help;

+ restructuring or reorganising to ensure the competence of staff taking on new health and safety responsibilities.

Control involves:

+ leading by example, demonstrating your commitment and letting everyone know that health and safety is important;

+ identifying people responsible for particular health and safety tasks, especially where special expertise is needed;

+ ensuring that managers, team leaders and all staff understand their responsibilities and have the time and resources to carry them out;

+ ensuring that everyone knows what to do and how they will be held accountable (e.g. by setting objectives).

Co-operation involves:

+ chairing your health and safety committee, if you have one, and consulting your staff and their representatives;

+ involving staff in planning and reviewing performance, written procedures and problem solving;

+ working with contractors who come onto your premises.

Communication involves:

+ providing information on hazards, risks and preventive measures to employees and contractors;

+ discussing health and safety on a regular basis;

+ being 'visible' on health and safety.

Monitoring and auditing performance

Setting standards helps to promote a positive culture and to control risks. The standards set out what staff will do to deliver the policy and identify who does what, when and the outcome. Standards must be:

+ measurable

+ achievable

+ realistic.

Standard statements must be measurable. Saying that 'staff must be trained' is difficult to measure if you can't say what is meant by training or who the staff are, in what they should be trained and by whom. If standards already exist, these can be adopted; if not, you will have to develop your own.

Standards that can be measured by audit have three main components:

+ structure – the resources and personnel available (quantity and quality)
  - staffing / skill mix
  - equipment required
  - documentation / records;

+ process – what you do with the resources to achieve your outcome;

+ outcome – the result of the effectiveness of the policy.

The National Standards provide a set of outcomes to be achieved by early years settings. Ofsted inspectors expect that child care providers will be able to show how they achieve each of the standards specific to their facility.

What an audit is and how to do it

Auditing is not a new idea and is practised in a variety of professions. The commonest approach to auditing is to set standards against which current practice can be measured and changes identified. This is often called the 'audit cycle', which is an ongoing process.

There are four components of an audit, which form the ongoing process that asks you to:

+ reflect on your performance;

+ observe your practice;

+ compare your practice to the accepted standard;

+ implement change.

The purpose of audit is to review current practice by using existing knowledge to improve the service provided. Its intention is to provide feedback to those involved and it is about the application of knowledge. Audit has a dual purpose of improving quality while educating and developing all those involved in the process. It should be seen as a learning process for both the organisation and individuals and needs to be conducted in an open manner.

Once an audit has been carried out, feedback of the results is useful for staff not only to understand the process but also to feel included. It can be useful to describe the positive things that came out of the audit along with areas that need improvement; individuals should not be criticised. Audit is not about staff appraisal but about improving the quality of service. Plenty of time should be given to discussion and to considering the recommendations that come out of the process.

Finally, once the results have been discussed, the audit process itself should be reviewed to identify three main areas:

+ What went well – look at the achievements; don't start with the negatives as focusing on the positive encourages staff morale.

✢ What was difficult – identify problems at each stage and how you tackled them; were the standardised checklists useful?

✢ What the next steps are – if it looks like you can't achieve your standard, what practical steps can you take to do so?

While it might be expected that changes need to be implemented, you may find that it is not always necessary. Audit may show that your standards are being met satisfactorily.

It is very easy to think of audit as a continuous cycle with a circle spinning round and round. However, this is not so. Audit is dynamic and revolves around providing a quality service with the purpose of improving the level of quality given. So you should be spiralling upwards, as the fundamental reason for undertaking audit is to improve the quality of service you provide to children and parents in your facility.

Best practice checklist

✢ Audit should not be judgemental; it looks at what is happening and can lead to informed decision making.

✢ Good planning makes for a successful audit.

✢ Setting local standards and criteria is an important part of making audit relevant to your own facility.

✢ Don't reinvent the wheel; make use of what is already available.

✢ Audit is a continuous process and is easier the second time around.

✢ Discuss the findings with all staff as this is a part of the process.

✢ Audit is not a circle but a spiral, and the loop is closed by re-auditing.

✢ Undertaking audit helps to improve the quality of care provided.

✢ Build a portfolio of evidence that shows compliance with national standards.

✢ A portfolio of evidence includes risk assessments, cleaning schedules, action plans, policies and procedures, minutes of meetings, parent information leaflets.

Get a copy of the 14 National Standards for under-eights day care, either by ordering it from the DfES Publications Centre on 0845 602 2260 or by downloading from the internet: www.surestart.gov.uk. Take one of the standards, look at the supporting criteria and draw up an action plan of how that standard can be achieved. Consider what evidence can be produced to show you can comply with the standard.

The following example looks at Standard 7: health (specifically 7.1 which relates to hygiene). An action plan has been started to show how it can be achieved and what evidence is needed to show compliance with the standard.

Standard statement	Supporting criteria	Action plan
The registered person promotes the good health of children and takes positive steps to prevent the spread of infection and appropriate measures when they are ill	Hygiene 7.1 the premises and equipment are clean	✛ List all furniture, fixtures and fittings and equipment that has to be cleaned ✛ Draw up a cleaning protocol for how everything should be cleaned ✛ State what cleaning products will be used ✛ State who will do the cleaning ✛ State the frequency with which the cleaning will be undertaken, e.g. daily, weekly, monthly ✛ List the protective clothing that needs to be worn for particular cleaning tasks

End-of-chapter summary

This chapter has provided an introduction to the issue of standards, audit and quality. Audit is a structured process that can be used to assess the quality of care given in the early years setting and can be a valuable source of insight as to how something is done. Done successfully, it can confirm that everyone is doing a good job and be a positive reinforcement of best practice.

CHAPTER 4

Individual policies and procedures

Introduction

A health and safety policy aims to influence all the activities undertaken in the early years setting, including the people, equipment and materials, and how work is structured. By providing a written policy that encompasses all aspects of health and safety, it shows to staff, parents and outside organisations that hazards have been identified and risks have been assessed, then either eliminated or controlled. This chapter covers the main areas of health and safety, including security, personal safety, fire, first aid, manual handling, electrical hazards, hazardous substances and such accidents as slips, trips and falls. Also included are audit tools to assist with the monitoring of the health and safety policy a self-review activity and a best practice checklist.

Security

Security is important: it aims to protect people and property from fire, theft, accident, loss of power, violent crime etc., 24 hours a day, without interfering with daily life. Security incidents may range from assault, trespass and use of offensive weapons to harassment, threatening or abusive behaviour and criminal acts of theft, burglary and vandalism. As with other aspects of health and safety, it is important to undertake a risk assessment to understand:

+ the type and scale of the risk;

+ trends or patterns in incidents involving your nursery;

+ security measures needed;

+ the efficiency of your chosen security measures;

+ how to prioritise within a realistic timeframe the additional controls identified in an action plan.

Having an identified contact in the local police force (such as the local crime prevention officer) can be helpful and such contacts can give advice about practical measures. There should be a system of recording and reporting incidents, even minor ones, so that they can be reviewed and used as a basis of information about the security measures needed.

Audit tool for security incidents in the early years setting

Date ....

Name of early years setting ....

Auditor ....

		Yes	No	N/A	Comments
1	There have been issues of trespass in the past 12 months				
2	There have been incidents of vandalism in the past 12 months				
3	There have been cases of theft and/or burglary in the past 12 months				
4	There have been arson attacks in the area in the past 12 months				
5	There has been a local problem of drug or solvent abuse in the past 12 months				

		Yes	No	N/A	Comments
6	There have been attacks/threats on staff and children in the past 12 months				
7	The early years setting is in a low crime rate area				
8	The early years setting is overlooked by busy roads or houses				
9	Boundaries are well defined, preventing intruders				
10	There are clear entrances with signs directing visitors				
11	Safe parking is available in well-lit area				
12	Building is well maintained				
13	It is not a multi-building site				
14	There are no areas for intruders to hide in unobserved				
15	All doors are secure				
16	Windows and roof-lights are protected against forced entry				
17	There are few computers, TVs, DVDs on the premises				
18	There is strong community and parent support				
19	There is a system for reporting suspicious incidents				
20	Waste and recycling bins are locked up every night				
21	There is security lighting of all entrances, footpaths and facades				
22	There is a system of surveillance, e.g. CCTV				
23	There is an intruder detector system on all ground floors				
24	There is a fire detection system				
25	All valuable property is marked and kept in a secure area				

Fire

While it is impossible to be totally immune to fire risk, early years settings can reduce the risk by implementing fire safety management.

Under the *Fire Precautions (Workplace) Regulations 1997* you must have an emergency plan, which should include the actions to be taken by staff if a fire occurs. It should also include any evacuation procedures and the arrangements for calling the fire brigade. A fire action notice should be clearly displayed in every room of the early years setting and a fire drill should be practised, preferably once a term.

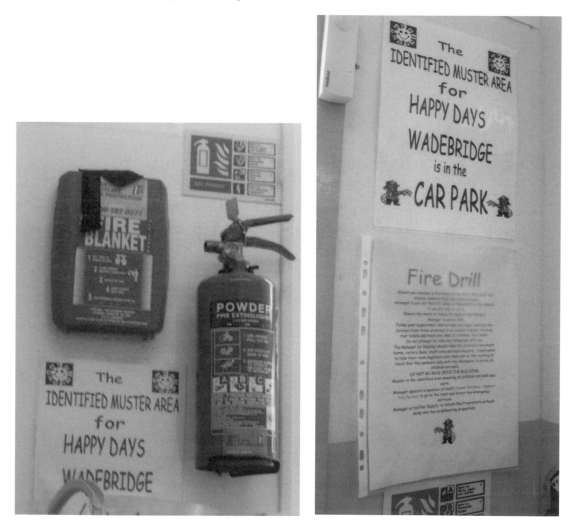

The responsibility for fire safety is usually shared between the governing body and the head of the early years setting and also the local education authority (LEA) where it maintains the early years setting. They must make sure that fire precautions comply with all relevant health and safety legislation. Advice on fire safety should be obtained from your local fire safety officer.

Fire safety management

The aim of fire safety management is to:

+ minimise the risk of fire;

+ protect the means of escape;

+ limit the spread of fire.

The main duties of fire safety management include:

+ undertaking hazard and risk assessments;

+ arranging training in fire safety;

+ producing an emergency plan and putting up fire notices;

+ conducting fire drills;

+ checking adequacy and maintenance of fire-fighting apparatus;

+ consulting the fire brigade and putting in place any recommendations;

+ conducting regular fire safety inspections;

+ making impromtu checks to ensure that fire safety rules are being followed;

+ making sure fire escape routes and fire exit doors and passageways are not obstructed and that doors open correctly;

+ ensuring that fire detection and protection systems are maintained and tested and keeping records of the tests;

+ making sure close-down procedures are followed;

+ including fire safety in regular health and safety reports to the governing body.

Audit tool for identifying fire hazards

Date .... Name of early years setting .... Auditor ....

		Yes	No	N/A	Comments
1	Staff are trained in evacuation procedures				
2	Fire action notices are displayed				
3	Fire practice drills are held on a regular basis				
4	Combustible materials are identified and stored correctly				
5	Fire doors are regularly inspected and maintained				
6	Fire doors are unlocked and available for immediate use at all times when the building is occupied				
7	Fire doors are identified with Fire Exit signs				
8	Portable electric or LPG heaters are not used				Replace naked flame and radiant heaters with fixed convectors or a central heating system
9	Tungsten filament bulbs are replaced with fluorescent fittings where there is a risk of combustible materials igniting				
10	Multi-point adapters are only used where it is unavoidable				Do not overload, provide additional sockets
11	Bins holding combustible waste are at least 10 metres away from any building, and either locked to a metal post or in a secure enclosure				

		Yes	No	N/A	Comments
12	Flammable wall and ceiling finishes have been removed or treated				
13	Display materials are kept to a minimum on escape routes or sprayed with fire retardant				
14	Highly flammable materials are stored in fire-resistant stores away from sources of ignition				
15	Ducts, chimneys and flues are kept clean and in good repair				
16	A 'hot work permit' system is operated and contractors and maintenance staff are provided with fire safety information				
17	A no-smoking policy is operated throughout the nursery				
18	All electrical inspection and testing is kept up to date and repairs are carried out promptly				
19	Only a competent nominated person wires plugs, using the correct fuse				
20	Faulty electrical equipment is immediately removed				
21	Flexes are kept as short as possible, equipment; with damaged cables is never used				
22	Staff know how to isolate the main electrical supply in an emergency				
23	Fire-fighting apparatus is placed in correct locations and tested annually				
24	Staff are trained in the use of different fire-fighting equipment				

Manual handling

The *Manual Handling Operations Regulations 1992* apply to a wide range of activities, work settings and loads. Manual handling injuries can happen wherever people work and many risk factors are involved. The Health and Safety Commission has prioritised the prevention and control of musculoskeletal injuries (MSI) but not all MSI injuries are preventable. Because of this it is important to encourage staff to report injuries early and access treatment and rehabilitation for those who do get injured. Employers have to consider the risks of manual handling to the health and safety of their staff and consult with them as to how such risks can be reduced.

Employers' responsibilities

+ Avoid the need for hazardous manual handling as far as is reasonably possible.

+ Assess the risk of injury from any hazardous manual handling that cannot be avoided.

+ Reduce the risk of injury from hazardous manual handling as far as is reasonably possible.

Employees' responsibilities

+ Follow appropriate systems of work for their safety.

+ Make proper use of equipment provided for their safety.

+ Co-operate with their employer on health and safety matters.

+ Tell their employer if they identify hazardous handling activities.

+ Take care to make sure that what they do does not put others at risk.

Assessing the risk

It is important not to create new hazards by changing practices.

+ Most situations will need simple observation to identify how to make things easier, less risky and less demanding.

+ Advice from outside experts may be helpful to get started or in difficult and unusual cases.

+ Keeping records of the main findings of assessments should always be done if it would be difficult to be repeated.

+ Records do not need to be kept if the assessment is easily repeated, because it is simple and obvious, or if the handling operations are low risk.

+ Generic assessments are acceptable where it is applicable to a number of staff.

+ Individual risk assessments may need to be carried out for employees with a disability, or those who become ill, are injured or return from a long period of sickness.

In all assessments it is important to identify all significant risks of injury and identify how to make practical improvements. Assessments should not be forgotten or filed away; the purpose of an assessment is to pinpoint the risks associated with the task and to prioritise in which order things should be improved. The assessment should be updated when significant changes are made in the workplace. Once risks have been identified, staff should be informed and the necessary measures taken to avoid or reduce them.

Moving and handling children

Staff need to be able to lift children correctly, both for their own safety and for that of the child.

+ Stand as close as possible to the child before you lift them and tell them what you are going to do. Keep your back straight and, bending your knees, hold the child firmly around their middle as you lift.

+ Be sure that there is nothing to hinder the lift, such as loose clothing catching on furniture or forgetting to undo a harness if the child is in a high chair.

+ Carry the child close to the body, as it reduces the strain on the back.

+ Only carry one child at a time unless there is a life-threatening emergency situation.

Electrical safety

Electricity can kill. Poor electrical installations and faulty electrical appliances can also lead to fires that may also cause death or injury to others. Electrical safety should be promoted at all times and careful planning and simple precautions can avoid most accidents.

The main hazards

The main hazards associated with electricity are:

+ contact with live parts causing shock and burns (normal mains voltage 230 volts AC can kill);

+ electrical faults leading to fires;

+ fire or explosion where electricity is the source of ignition in a potentially flammable or explosive atmosphere.

The risk of injury from electricity is linked to where and how it is used and the risks are greater:

+ in wet surroundings;

+ out of doors;

+ in cramped spaces with a lot of earthed metalwork.

Risk assessment

Following a risk assessment certain precautions should be taken as an example of good practice to reduce the risks.

Connections

+ Plugs and sockets should be sited beyond children's reach wherever possible.

+ Childproof caps and plugs should always be used.

+ Plugs and sockets should fit firmly, needing some force to insert and remove them.

+ Disconnect, mark and report any plugs or sockets that form a connection that is warm to the touch. Do not use them until they have been repaired or replaced.

✚ Always grasp the plug to remove it from the socket – never pull the flex.

Equipment

✚ All electrical equipment should be properly tested and carry an annual test certificate (PAT certificate for portable electrical equipment).

✚ Only a competent electrician should make repairs on electrical equipment and wiring.

Flexes

✚ Check flexes frequently for fraying, bare wires and other defects. Pay particular attention to the point where the flex attaches to the equipment.

✚ Keep flexes away from oil, grease or any material that causes deterioration.

✚ Keep flexes out of the way so that they do not become tripping hazards or get damaged by people walking on them.

✚ Avoid using extension leads and never overload them. Never use extension leads around children.

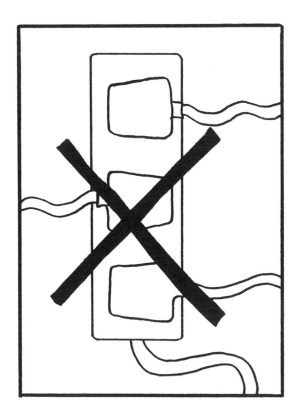

Prevention

A system of preventative maintenance should be followed to prevent any injuries. This should include a visual inspection and, where necessary, testing of equipment. Most electrical risks within the nursery can be controlled by concentrating on a simple, inexpensive system of looking for visible signs of damage or faults. This needs to be backed up by testing as necessary and records of tests and results of inspections should be kept.

Audit for electrical safety

Date ....

Name of early years setting ....

Auditor ....

		Yes	No	N/A	Comments
1	Plugs and sockets are sited beyond children's reach wherever possible				
2	Childproof caps and plugs are used				
3	Plugs and sockets fit firmly, needing force to insert and remove them				
4	Any plugs and sockets that are warm to the touch are disconnected, marked and reported				Do not use them until they have been repaired or replaced.
5	Plugs are always grasped to remove them from the sockets, never pulled by the flex				
6	All electrical equipment is properly tested and carries an annual test certificate				
7	Only competent electricians make repairs on electrical equipment and wiring				
8	Flexes are checked frequently for fraying, bare wires and other defects				
9	Flexes are kept away from oil, grease or any material that causes deterioration				
10	Flexes are kept out of the way so they do not become tripping hazards or get damaged by people walking on them				
11	Extension leads are rarely used and never overloaded				

Slips, trips and falls

Risk factors to consider

Some of the risk factors to consider are:

+ environmental – floors, steps, slopes, etc.;

+ contamination – by water, food, litter, etc.;

+ organisational – task, safety culture;

+ footwear – a 'sensible shoe' policy;

+ individual factors – supervision, pedestrian behaviour, information and training.

Changes to consider

Changes to consider include:

+ changing surfaces to slip-resistant flooring;

+ cleaning spillages immediately;

+ routine cleaning of floors, choice of cleaning products and allowing floors to dry thoroughly before use;

+ establishing a 'sensible shoe' policy – flat shoes that enclose the whole foot – for staff and children;

+ improving lighting to make any hazards visible.

Employers have to consider the individual needs of their children and staff and visitors who may have disabilities. Things to consider are events such as open days, when people who are unfamiliar with the premises will be visiting.

Many slip incidents happen in kitchens and food serving areas, so consideration should be given to work surfaces and appropriate flooring here. Any catering or cleaning contractors should have an agreement with the employer as to how the work will be carried out and describing the precautions they will take to reduce the risk of any slip or trip injury occurring. The issues to discuss include:

+ What equipment should or should not be used;

✚ what personal protective equipment should be used and who will provide it;

✚ working procedures;

✚ number of people to do the work;

✚ reporting of incidents and keeping records.

Clearning

There should be detailed information on how staff will manage the cleaning of spillages and the routine cleaning of floors. Wet cleaning can leave a very thin layer of cleaning solution on the floor that can take up to five minutes to dry, resulting in very slippery conditions.

Footwear policy

Footwear is an important part of preventing slip incidents and a 'sensible shoe' policy for everyone can make a significant reduction in slip and trip injuries. This means wearing flat shoes that enclose the entire foot, not sandals or sling-back shoes.

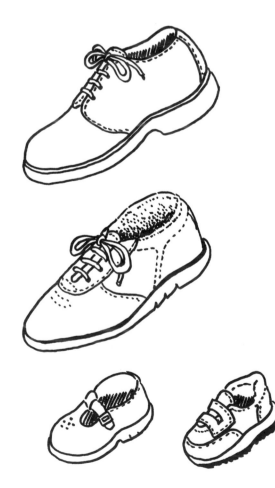

Lighting

Lighting is very important as poor lighting can obscure any hazards, while excessively bright light can cause glare, which again obscures hazards.

Changes to the environment

Where changes or modifications to premises are made, consideration should always be given to reducing and eliminating slip and trip risks in the design stage, such as installing slip-resistant flooring. Adequate facilities have to be provided in buildings for the storage and drying of children's outdoor clothing and for the storage of their other belongings under the *Education (School Premises) Regulations 1999*.

Audit for slips, trips and falls

Date
....

Name of early years setting
....

Auditor
....

		Yes	No	N/A	Comments
1	External steps, paths and parking areas are suitable for the amount of use, have flat even surfaces and are kept free of mud, leaves and snow				
2	Edges of steps are marked using an anti-slip coating				
3	Lights are replaced, repaired or cleaned before levels of lighting become too low to be safe in outside areas				
4	Playground surfaces are flat and well maintained to avoid surface water				
5	Adequate supervision is provided in playgrounds at all times				
6	Suitable non-slip, water-absorbing mats are provided at entrances				
7	Hidden steps and changes of level at entrances and exits have displayed warning signs				
8	Warning signs are displayed where there is a risk of slipping				

		Yes	No	N/A	Comments
9	Where appropriate, anti-slip coating is applied to areas of smooth flooring in internal stairs and corridors that may become wet				
10	Handrails are provided for internal stairs				
11	Edges of internal stairs are marked with anti-slip coating				
12	Internal lights are replaced, repaired or cleaned before levels of lighting become too low to be safe on stairs and in corridors				
13	Storage racks are provided for children's bags and outdoor wear				
14	Children's practical work is safely displayed				
15	Toys are cleared away and stored safely after use				
16	Staff wear suitable footwear in kitchen and food preparation areas				
17	All spillages are cleaned immediately				
18	Suitable floor surface is provided in kitchen and food preparation areas				
19	Warning signs are displayed when cleaning is in progress				
20	All floors are cleaned and dried effectively				
21	All floors are cleaned after children have eaten				
22	There are no trailing cables				
23	Good housekeeping is maintained				
24	Worn or damaged carpets/tiles are replaced				

First aid and reporting accidents

First aid can save lives and prevent minor injuries from becoming major ones. Under health and safety legislation, employers have to make sure that there are adequate and appropriate equipment, facilities and personnel for providing first aid in the workplace. People at work can fall ill or suffer injuries and it doesn't matter whether or not they are caused by the work they do. What is important is that they receive immediate attention and an ambulance is called for in serious cases.

It is up to the employer to decide what is considered to be appropriate and adequate for their workplace and they have to assess what their first-aid needs are.

First-aid provision

The minimum first-aid provision is:

✚ a suitably stocked first-aid box;

✚ an appointed person to take charge of first-aid arrangements;

✚ information for employees on first-aid arrangements;

✚ a qualified first-aider on duty at all times when children are present – whether in the setting or on an outing.

The *Management of Health and Safety at Work Regulations 1992* require employers to undertake a suitable and sufficient assessment of the risks to the health and safety of their employees at work. The first-aid needs should be reviewed on a regular basis, at least annually, especially if there have been any changes, to make sure that the provision is adequate.

All staff must be informed of the first-aid arrangements within the early years setting. This can be achieved by:

+ displaying first-aid notices stating the location of equipment, facilities, the names of the first-aid personnel and the procedures for monitoring and reviewing the nursery's first-aid needs;

+ displaying the notices in a prominent place throughout the nursery, at least one in each building if the nursery is on several sites;

+ including first-aid information on induction programmes for new staff and in staff handbooks and information for parents.

Staff should hold an appropriate first-aid certificate in paediatric first aid; this can be achieved by undertaking the paediatric first-aid course 'First Aid in Early Years Settings', which also provides them with the status of an appointed person. This course is approved by Ofsted, NSPCC, PLA, NCMA, BTEC and CACHE.

Assessment of first-aid provision

Points to consider	Actions to take
What are the significant risks in your workplace; what are the risks of injury or ill health? Are there any specific risks, e.g. working with hazardous substances?	You will need to consider: + specific training for first-aiders + extra first-aid equipment + precise siting of first-aid equipment
What is your record of accidents and cases of ill health? What type are they and where did they happen?	You may need to: + make provision in certain areas + review the contents of the first-aid box
How many staff are employed?	You must have a qualified first-aider available in the setting at all times

Are there inexperienced staff on the site, employees with disabilities or special health problems?	You will need to consider: ✚ special equipment ✚ local siting of equipment
What is the size of the nursery? Is it on split sites or levels?	You will need to consider additional provision for first aid in each building or on each floor
Is there shift work or out-of-hours working?	First-aid provision has to be available at all times people are at work
Is the nursery remote from the local emergency services?	It is good practice to inform the local emergency services, in writing, of the nursery's location (with Ordnance Survey grid references if necessary) and information that might affect access to the nursery. If there is more than one entrance, clear instructions should be given as to where or to whom they should report.
Do your staff travel far to work or work alone?	You will need to consider: ✚ providing personal first-aid kits and training staff in how to use them ✚ giving personal communications to staff
Do you have any work-experience trainees?	First-aid provision must cover them as well as other staff

What is an appointed person?

An appointed person is someone who is chosen to:

✚ take charge when someone is injured or ill, including calling an ambulance if needed;

✚ look after first-aid equipment, such as restocking the first-aid box.

Appointed persons should not try to give first aid for which they have not been trained, but short emergency first-aid courses are available. It is good practice to make sure that the appointed person has emergency first-aid training and refresher training as appropriate. There is a Level 2 first aid paediatric course that covers, among other things:

+ what to do in an emergency;

+ cardiopulmonary resuscitation;

+ first aid for the unconscious casualty;

+ first aid for the wounded or bleeding.

Emergency first-aid training should help an appointed person to cope with an emergency, improving their competence and confidence.

It may be necessary to appoint more than one person to this role to cover the working hours of the premises. In an early years setting a first-aider must be on duty at all times.

What is a first-aider?

A first-aider is someone who has undergone training to provide first aid at work and has a current First Aid at Work certificate. **The training has to be approved by the Health and Safety Executive (HSE)** and lists of first-aid training organisations in your area are available from them. The 12-hour Level 2 paediatric course is advisable. Ensure that any training organisation is informed of the ages of children that you care for so that they can provide appropriate training to cover young children and babies, as the requirements are very different from those for adults, especially in resuscitation.

The main duties of a first-aider are to:

+ give immediate help to those with common injuries or illnesses and those arising from specific hazards in the nursery;

+ make sure that an ambulance or other professional medical help is called when necessary.

Unless it is part of their contact of employment, staff agreeing to become first-aiders do so on a voluntary basis. When selecting someone to undertake the role of first-aider, you should consider:

+ reliability and communication skills;

+ aptitude and ability to absorb new knowledge and learn new skills;

+ ability to cope with stressful and physically demanding emergency procedures;

+ normal duties – they must be able to leave immediately to attend to an emergency.

The minimum requirement is that an appointed person must take charge of the first-aid arrangements, and the number of appointed persons needed has to be decided by the employer, following the risk assessment. Cover must be available at all times that people are on the premises.

Employers should make sure that their insurance arrangements provide full cover for claims arising from actions of staff acting within the scope of their employment. Those early years settings that come under the local education authority (LEA) should consult with them about their insurance arrangements.

Keeping qualifications up to date

First-aiders must hold a valid certificate of competence issued by an organisation that is approved by the HSE.

+ First Aid at Work certificates are valid for only three years.

+ Employers should arrange refresher courses and refreshing of competence before certificates expire.

+ If an individual's certificate expires they will have to undertake another full course.

+ Refresher courses can be arranged up to three months before the expiry date and the new certificate takes effect from the date of expiry.

+ Early years settings should keep a record of first-aiders and certification dates.

First-aid materials, equipment and facilities

Employers must provide proper materials, equipment and facilities at all times. First-aid equipment must be clearly labelled and easily accessible.

First-aid containers

+ There should be at least one fully stocked first-aid container for each setting. The assessment should include the number of first-aid containers.

+ Additional first-aid containers will be needed for split sites, high risk areas and any off-site activities such as outings.

+ All first-aid containers must be marked with a white cross on a green background.

+ Where you place first-aid containers should be given careful consideration – if possible they should be kept near to hand-washing facilities.

+ All staff should know where the first-aid box is placed and it should be clearly visible and marked.

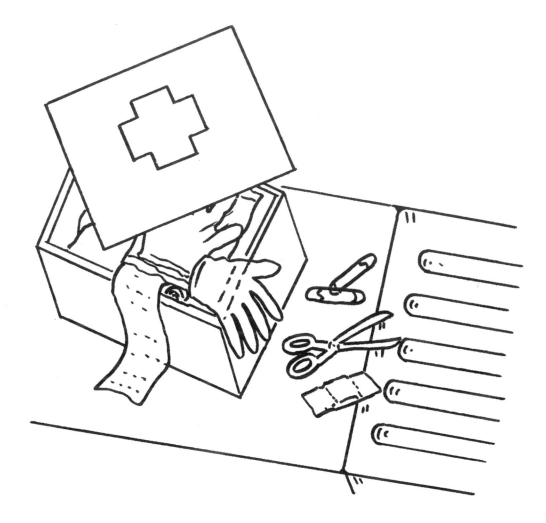

Contents of a first-aid container

There is no set list of items to keep in a first-aid box as it depends upon how needs are assessed. The HSE recommends a minimum stock of first-aid items, to include:

+ a leaflet giving general guidance on first aid;

+ twenty individually wrapped sterile adhesive dressings (assorted sizes);

+ two sterile eye pads;

+ four individually wrapped triangular bandages (preferably sterile);

- six safety pins;

- six-medium sized (12 cm x 12 cm) individually wrapped sterile unmedicated wound dressings;

- two large (18 cm x 18 cm) sterile individually wrapped unmedicated wound dressings;

- one pair of disposable gloves.

Other equipment that is appropriate for the setting should be kept nearby and can include:

- disposable plastic aprons;

- scissors;

- eye protection;

- spillage kit for body fluids.

Tablets and medicines must not be kept in the first-aid box.

The first-aid procedures should identify the person responsible for maintaining the contents of the container, which should be checked frequently and restocked after use. Keep a record sheet to be signed each time the kit is checked and restocked.

Travelling first-aid containers

First-aid container should be provided for off-site visits and the nursery manager should assess the level of first-aid provision needed.

The HSE recommend that where there is no special risk identified, a minimum stock of first-aid items for travelling first-aid containers is:

- a leaflet giving general advice on first aid;

- six individually wrapped sterile adhesive dressings;

- one large sterile unmedicated wound dressing (18 cm x 18 cm);

- two triangular bandages;

- two safety pins;

- individually wrapped moist cleansing wipes;

- one pair of disposable gloves.

Other useful items to include and carry are:

+ bottled sterile water;

+ soap and water cleansing wipes.

Transport regulations

Transport regulations require that all minibuses and public service vehicles used have on board a first-aid container with the following items:

+ ten antiseptic wipes, foil packaged;

+ one conforming disposable bandage (not less than 7.5 cm wide);

+ two triangular bandages;

+ one packet of 24 assorted adhesive dressings;

+ three large sterile unmedicated ambulance dressings (not less than 15 cm x 20 cm);

+ two sterile eye pads with attachments;

+ twelve assorted safety pins;

+ one pair of rustless blunt-ended scissors.

The first-aid container has to be:

+ maintained in a good condition;

+ suitable for the purpose of keeping the items in a good condition (i.e. rustproof, dustproof and damp-proof);

+ readily available for use;

+ marked as a first-aid container.

Infection control precautions

All staff should take precautions to prevent infection and follow basic hygiene procedures. Personal protective equipment should be provided, which includes the use of single-use disposable gloves and plastic aprons when handling blood or body fluids. Hand-washing facilities should be easily accessible and used dressings and bandages should be disposed of safely as clinical waste.

First-aid records

It is a legal requirement to keep records of accidents at work in a book of any incidents involving injuries or illness which have happened. Any information recorded must comply with the *Data Protection Act 1998* and managers should be aware of the recent *Freedom of Information Act 2000* and the *Freedom of Information (Scotland) Act 2002*, which affect all public authorities.

The following information should be recorded:

+ date, time and place of injury;

+ name and job of injured or ill person;

+ details of injury/illness and any first aid given;

+ what happened to the casualty immediately afterwards (went home/hospital, etc.);

+ name and signature of the person who dealt with the incident.

Reporting accidents

Some accidents must be reported to the HSE and in 1996 the law changed to incorporate two new changes into the reporting requirements. These were that the definition of an 'accident' now includes an act of non-consensual physical violence to staff, and the simplification of reporting certain accidents to people who are not at work, e.g. children.

+ Employers who have ten or more members of staff must keep readily accessible records in either a written or electronic format for a minimum of three years.

+ Where the local authority is the employer, the early years setting should follow their LEA's procedures as they may wish you to report directly to them centrally for insurance or statistical purposes.

Early years settings must inform Ofsted of the following:

+ an outbreak of infectious disease that is considered sufficiently serious by a registered medical practitioner;

+ any serious injury to, or serious illness or death of, any child or other person on the premises;

+ any allegations of serious harm against, or abuse of, a child by any person looking after children, or living, working or employed at the premises;

+ any serious matter or event that is likely to affect the welfare of any child on the premises.

Under the *Reporting of Injuries, Diseases and Dangerous Occurrences Regulations 1995* some accidents must be reported to the HSE. Fatal and major injuries and dangerous occurrences must be notified immediately (e.g. by telephone) and followed up within ten days with a written report. Other incidents must be reported to the HSE within ten days.

It is important to remember that for most employers a reportable accident, dangerous occurrence or case of disease is a comparatively rare event. It is, however, a legal requirement to report it when it does occur.

Audit for first aid

Date

....

Name of early years setting

....

Auditor

....

		Yes	No	N/A	Comments
1	There is an appointed person available to take charge of first-aid arrangements				
2	There is a suitably stocked first-aid box				
3	Records are kept of all accidents and emergencies				
4	The local emergency services have been provided with the location of the nursery				
5	The appointed person has undertaken an emergency first-aid training course including resuscitation of children				
6	All first-aiders have undertaken a recognised HSE training course including first aid for children				
7	First-aid provision is reviewed on an annual basis				
8	First-aid notices including names of first-aiders or appointed person on duty, are displayed appropriately in the nursery				
9	First aid is included in staff induction and annual updates				
10	Specific first-aid hazards have been identified in the assessment process				
11	First Aid at Work certificates are current and up to date				
12	All first-aid boxes are marked with a white cross on a green background				
13	Travelling first-aid boxes are available for off-site activities				
14	Personal protective equipment of disposable gloves and aprons is provided				
15	Hand-washing facilities are available				

Workplace violence and personal safety

It is good practice to have a general policy on workplace violence that includes ways to minimise its occurrence. It should include:

✚ staff training;

✚ the working environment;

✚ maintenance of adequate staffing levels;

✚ back-up procedures for emergencies.

Training should include:

✚ personal safety training;

✚ recognising signs that could lead to aggressive behaviour;

✚ using techniques to calm situations and potential assailants.

Types of incidents include:

✚ *Assault* – any intentional or reckless act that causes someone to fear or expect immediate unlawful force or personal violence.

✚ *Battery* – the intentional or reckless infliction of unlawful force or personal violence.

The two offences may occur together and, in all but minor cases, early years settings should refer any assaults that appear to involve actual bodily harm to the police.

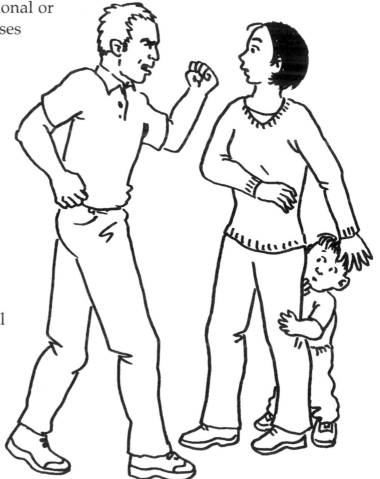

Best practice checklist

+ Have a health and safety plan.

+ Always consider health and safety before any new activity is started.

+ Identify all hazards in the workplace and assess risks to staff, children and visitors.

+ Have emergency plans and practise evacuation procedures.

+ Provide training for staff on all aspects of health and safety, both on starting work and in annual updates.

+ Standards put in place should be reviewed and updated regularly.

SELF-REVIEW ACTIVITY

Using the table for slip and trip risk control measures, look around your area of work and consider whether you have similar measures in place.

Discuss your findings with colleagues and decide whether the audit tool needs to be adapted to reflect your premises' activities and how you answered the questions. Does it identify gaps in staff knowledge and do policies need to be reviewed and updated?

Slip and trip risk control

Area	Practical control measures
External steps, paths and parking areas	+ Replace, repair or clean lights before lighting levels become too low to be safe + Ensure steps and paths are suitable for the amount of pedestrian traffic + Make sure paving slabs are secure and tarmac paths give a flat even surface + Make sure parking areas are free of potholes + Mark the edge of steps using an anti-slip coating, as smooth gloss paint will give a slippery surface when wet + Where appropriate, provide handrails and keep them in good condition + Discourage short cuts across grassed and muddy areas

Area	Practical control measures
	✚ Clean leaves and mud from surfaces ✚ Remove algal growth from surfaces ✚ Have procedures in place to deal with snow and ice
Playgrounds	✚ Ensure surfaces are flat and well maintained to avoid surface water ✚ Remove accumulation of mud/water/algae ✚ Make sure appropriate footwear is worn by users ✚ Provide adequate supervision at all times
Entrances and exits	✚ Provide suitable non-slip, water-absorbing mats at entrances ✚ Maintain mats in good condition and change when saturated ✚ Make sure that temporary matting does not pose a trip risk ✚ Display warning signs of hidden steps and changes of level ✚ Where appropriate display warning signs of the risk of slipping ✚ Place door catches and door stops safely
Internal stairs and corridors	✚ Make sure that there is a staggered release of children into heavily used traffic routes ✚ Have measures in place for the flow of traffic up and down stairs and along corridors ✚ Mark the edges of stairs with anti-slip coating ✚ Provide handrails ✚ Replace, repair or clean lights before lighting levels become too low to be safe ✚ Where appropriate, apply anti-slip coating to areas of smooth flooring that may become wet
Classroom areas (including baby room and practical areas)	✚ Provide storage racks for children's bags and outdoor wear ✚ Consider anti-slip flooring in potentially wet areas, such as under coat hooks or where water play is undertaken ✚ Do not store materials or equipment below tables and benches ✚ Avoid overcrowding of rooms ✚ Control the entry and exit of people from classes ✚ Display children's practical work safely

Area	Practical control measures
	✚ Clear away toys when no longer in use ✚ Remove floor contamination as soon as possible ✚ Provide suitable storage for goods and equipment
Kitchens and food preparation areas (including baby food)	✚ Staff should wear suitable footwear ✚ Provide suitable equipment to avoid spillages from cooking and washing, etc. ✚ Ensure good ventilation to avoid steam, smoke and condensation ✚ Clean spillages and pick up food contamination immediately ✚ Use safe cleaning methods ✚ Provide suitable floor surface ✚ Clean floors and dry floors effectively ✚ Ensure good housekeeping around waste bins ✚ Display suitable warning signs when cleaning is in progress ✚ Remove warning signs once cleaning/drying has been completed
Dining areas	✚ Staff should wear suitable footwear ✚ Clean spillages immediately ✚ Use safe cleaning methods ✚ Provide suitable flooring ✚ Clean floors after children have eaten ✚ Display suitable warning signs when cleaning is in progress ✚ Remove warning signs once cleaning/drying has been completed
Offices	✚ Avoid trailing cables ✚ Provide adequate storage; avoid using the floor ✚ Encourage good housekeeping around photocopiers, printers, etc. ✚ Replace worn or damaged carpets/tiles ✚ Provide secure storage for bags, etc.
Educational visits	✚ Assess location and anticipated weather ✚ Modify the visit depending upon local conditions when on site ✚ Wear suitable footwear ✚ Ensure effective management of the visit

Area	Practical control measures
Toilets/nappy-changing/waste and laundry areas	+ Provide suitable flooring for these areas + Provide appropriate clinical waste containers + Hand-washing facilities should be available + Laundry facilities should be separate from catering facilities + Ensure suitable cleaning frequencies for toilets, nappy-changing area and sinks

End-of-chapter summary

This chapter has reviewed the different subject areas to be included in a health and safety policy. Having a written policy is never enough; it is important to be able to measure whether the precautions you have implemented have been successful. Such monitoring should be an active process that does not rely upon reacting to accidents or to occasions when things go wrong. Undertaking audits by yourself or outside agencies tells you about the reliability and effectiveness of your systems.

Promoting health and safety to parents

Step-by-step advice to parents

Getting the balance between encouraging children to explore their world and making sure they don't hurt themselves is difficult to achieve. Developing the skills that as adults we take for granted takes time. The following guidance can make the home a safer place for everyone.

Photocopy the following information sheets and display them in a place where parents can read them. For greater impact, allow the children to colour them in first.

SAFETY IN THE HOME – THE KITCHEN

Hazards

! Burns and scalds

! Fire

! Falls and slipping

! Lacerations

! Poisoning

! Electrocution

Recommendations

● In the kitchen use child-resistant locks, especially on the cutlery drawer and where poisonous cleaning fluids are kept

● Use a stable childproof barrier at the entrance of the kitchen to reduce access to the hazards in the kitchen while still allowing supervision

● Do not leave a baby unattended on any raised surface, even strapped in a car seat on the kitchen table

● Install a non-slip surface for the floor to reduce the risk of falls and slipping

● Install smoke alarms near the entrance to the kitchen and have fire safety devices (fire blanket and extinguisher) in the kitchen

● Fit thermostatic mixing valve to the hot water tap to reduce the risk of scalding

● Keep hot drinks, food, kettles and pan handles out of reach of children

● Keep medicines and cleaning products out of sight and reach of children

● Ensure the cables of electrical appliances are out of reach

SAFETY IN THE HOME – THE BATHROOM

Hazards

! Drowning

! Scalds

! Falls and slipping

! Poisoning from fluids or medicines

! Children climbing out of windows

Recommendations

● Have a thermostatic mixing valve fitted to your bath's hot tap. If you don't have one, **always** put cold water into the bath first and then add hot water. Test the temperature of bath water with your elbow

● Never leave a baby or young child in the bath, even with an older sister or brother

● Install a non-slip surface for the floor to reduce the risk of falls and slipping

● Make sure any glass used for mirrors is safety glass

● Fit child-resistant catches to prevent children accessing toiletries or medicines. Use child-proof bottles

SAFETY IN THE HOME – THE GARDEN

Hazards

! Children running onto the road

! Drowning in ponds or other water features

! Garden furniture and tools or play equipment

Recommendations

● Make sure garden gates are self-closing and self-latching and have childproof locks

● Keep the garden area separate from the driveway

● Keep garden tools and chemicals separate from children's bikes and play equipment and locked securely away

● Cover any ponds with secure safety covers **or** replace ponds with sandpits until children are older

● Do not plant toxic or poisonous plants in the garden

● Never leave a child unattended in the garden

SAFETY IN THE HOME – LIVING AREAS

Hazards

! Falls and trips

! Burns and scalds

! Accidents

! Suffocation

! Electrocution

Recommendations

● Fit safety gates at the top and bottom of stairs and window locks and safety catches that stop windows opening more than 6.5 cm (2.5 inches)

● Do not use a baby walker – babies learn to walk in their own time

● Use a fire guard for all types of fires, whether they are solid fuel, electric or gas

● Fit smoke alarms and carbon monoxide (CO) alarms in your home and check that they work correctly every month. Be prepared – plan for how you would escape if there is a fire in the house

● CAPT and RoSPA recommend that the top bunk of bunk beds is not used by children under the age of six years as safety standards are based on the average measurements for children this age

● Use angle braces or anchors to attach furniture to the wall so that children can't pull it over onto themselves

● Once a baby starts to pull themselves up in the cot, remove mobiles, etc. to remove the risk of strangulation or choking

● Always put a baby to sleep on their back and remove soft bedding until the baby is one year old

● Do not leave a baby unattended on a changing table

SAFETY IN THE HOME – MISCELLANEOUS

Hazards

! Choking

! Strangulation

! Car travel

Recommendations

● Keep small coins and toys out of reach so children do not put them in their mouth

● Do not leave a baby alone with a feeding bottle

● Avoid clothes that have drawstrings, ribbons and toys that have long strings

● Use the right child car seat for the age and weight of the child. Seat belts are designed for adults, not children

● Never fit rear-facing baby seats in the front passenger seat of the car if a passenger air bag is fitted

● It is safer for children to be carried in the back of the car and any child under the age of 14 years must be properly restrained

● You can only carry a child under the age of three in the front seat of the car if they are in a child car seat. Over three years, if there is no child car seat you must use the adult seat belt

Template of a health and safety policy

(based on leaflet provided by HSE to small businesses)

Health and Safety Policy Statement

Health and Safety at Work etc. Act 1974

This is the Health and Safety Policy Statement of [insert name of early years setting]...

Our statement of general policy is to:

[insert aims of the early years setting on health and safety]

....

....

....

Signature [name of employer]..

Date...

Review date...

<u>Responsibilities</u>

Overall and final responsibility for health and safety [insert employer's name]
....

Day-to-day responsibility is delegated to [insert name if applicable]
....

The following staff have responsibility in the following areas [insert name
and area/topic of responsibility]..

....

....

All staff have to co-operate on health and safety matters and not interfere
with anything provided to safeguard their health and safety. They must at all
times take reasonable care of their own health and safety and report any
concerns to an appropriate person as agreed in this policy statement.

Health and safety risks arising from work activities

Risk assessments are carried out by [insert name]

....

Findings of risk assessments are reported to [insert name]

....

Actions to be taken to remove and/or control risks are approved by [insert name of person responsible] ....

.... [insert name] will be responsible for making sure that any action is implemented and that they have removed and/or reduced the risks identified

Risk assessments are reviewed every [insert timeframe] ....
or when activities change, whichever is the earliest..................................

....

Consultation with staff

Staff representative(s) are [insert name(s) of person(s) responsible]

....

....

Safe equipment

.... [insert name] is responsible for identifying all equipment requiring maintenance

.... [insert name] is responsible for making sure effective maintenance procedures are drawn up

.... [insert name] is responsible for making sure that all identified maintenance is implemented

Any problems found should be reported to [insert name of person responsible] ....

.... [insert name] will check that any new plant and equipment meets health and safety standards before purchase

Safe handling and use of substances

.... [insert name] is responsible for identifying all substances that need a COSHH assessment

.... [insert name] is responsible for doing the COSHH assessments

.... [insert name] is responsible for making sure that all actions identified are implemented

.... [insert name] is responsible for making sure that all relevant staff are told about the COSHH assessments

.... [insert name] will check that new substances can be used safely before they are purchased

Risk assessments are reviewed every [insert timeframe] .... or when activities change, whichever is the earliest

Information, instruction and supervision

The Health and Safety Law poster is displayed at [insert location] .... and leaflets are available from [insert name of person responsible] ....

Health and safety advice is available from [insert name of person responsible] ....

Supervision of young workers/trainees will be undertaken/arranged/ monitored by [insert name of person responsible] ....

.... [insert name] is responsible for making sure that staff working at locations under the control of other employers are provided with relevant health and safety information

Competency for tasks and training

Induction training is provided for all staff by [insert name of person responsible] ....

Job-specific training is provided by [insert name of person responsible] ....

List of jobs needing special training are [insert job roles] ....

Training records are kept [Insert location and name of person responsible] ....

Training is identified, arranged and monitored by [insert name of person responsible] ....

Accidents, first aid and work-related ill health

Health surveillance is required for staff undertaking the following jobs [insert job roles]..
....

Health surveillance is arranged by [insert name] ....

Health surveillance records are kept [insert location and name] ....
....

First-aid box(es) are kept [insert location]..

The appointed person(s)/first-aider(s) are [insert name(s)]..........................
....

All accidents and incidents of work-related illness are recorded in the accident book, which is kept by [insert name of person responsible and where it is kept] ....
....

.... [insert name] is responsible for reporting accidents, diseases and dangerous occurrences under RIDDOR to the enforcing authority

Emergency procedures, fire, flood, bomb scare and evacuation

.... [insert name] is responsible for making sure the fire risk assessment is carried out and implemented

Escape routes are checked by [insert name of person responsible and when it is done]..

Alarms are tested by [insert name of person responsible and when it is done]...

Emergency evacuation will be tested every [insert frequency]...........................

Monitoring

To check the working conditions and make sure that safe working practices are being followed, we will [insert your procedures, e.g. spot check visits, investigating any accidents or ill health]

....

....

....

Risk assessment

[insert your risk assessment]

Bibliography

Department for Education and Employment (1996) *Education (School Premises) Regulations 1996*. London: HMSO.

Department for Education and Skills (2003) *National Standards for Under 8s Day Care and Childminding*. Nottingham: DfES Publications.

Great Britain (1990) *Food Safety Act 1990*. London: HMSO.

Great Britain (1991) *Food Premises (Registration) Regulations 1991*. London: HMSO.

Great Britain (1995) *Food Safety (General Food Hygiene) Regulations 1995*. London: HMSO.

Great Britain (1995) *Food Safety (Temperature Control) Regulations 1995*. London: HMSO.

Great Britain (1999) *Foods Standards Act 1999*. London: The Stationery Office.

Great Britain (2000) *Freedom of Information Act 2000 for England, Wales and Northern Ireland*. London: The Stationery Office.

Great Britain (2002) *Freedom of Information (Scotland) Act 2002*. London: The Stationery Office.

Health and Safety Commission (1969) *Employers' Liability (Compulsory Insurance) Act 1969*. London: HMSO.

Health and Safety Commission (1981) *Health and Safety (First Aid) Regulations 1981*. London: HMSO.

Health and Safety Commission (1989) *Electricity at Work Regulations 1989*. London: HMSO.

Health and Safety Commission (1989) *Health and Safety Information for Employees Regulations 1989*. London: HMSO.

Health and Safety Commission (1989) *Noise at Work Regulations 1989*. London: HMSO.

Health and Safety Commission (1992) *Health and Safety (Display Screen Equipment) Regulations 1992*. London: HMSO.

Health and Safety Commission (1992) *Manual Handling Operations Regulations 1992*. London: HMSO.

Health and Safety Commission (1992) *Personal Protective Equipment at Work Regulations 1992*. London: HMSO.

Health and Safety Commission (1992) *Workplace (Health, Safety and Welfare) Regulations 1992*. London: HMSO.

Health and Safety Commission (1995) *Reporting of Injuries, Diseases and Dangerous Occurrences Regulations 1995* (RIDDOR). London: HMSO.

Health and Safety Commission (1998) *Provision and Use of Work Equipment Regulations 1998*. London: The Stationery Office.

Health and Safety Commission (1999) *Fire Precautions (Workplace) (Amendment) Regulations 1999*. London: The Stationery Office.

Health and Safety Commission (1999) *Management of Health and Safety at Work Regulations 1999*. London: The Stationery Office.

Health Service Advisory Committee (1974) *Health and Safety at Work etc. Act 1974*, London: HMSO.

Health and Safety Commission (2002) *Control of Substances Hazardous to Health Regulations 2002* (COSHH). London: The Stationery Office.

Maxwell, R. (1984) 'Quality assessment in health'. *British Medical Journal*, 288: 1470–2.

Index